M000113329

THIS NOTEBOOK BELONGS TO ....

CONTACT ....